MY LIFE IN POETRY

MY LIFE IN POETRY

POETRY

Volume 1

PRUDENCE ANN SMITH MD FACR

ISBN: 0692610294
ISBN 13: 9780692610299
Library of Congress Control Number: 2015921474
Belle Publishers: Tulare, CA

Letters of Life
Dedication
To my beloved, my guide

To you
Of whom my words are but a dim reflection,
And never can capture
The beauty of your soul,
To you,
Who are my every dream fulfilled,
To you,
Whose love has made me whole.

TABLE OF CONTENTS

MY LOVE FOR YOU

Your warmth is my jewel,
Your love is my treasure,
It's wealth beyond words
And joy beyond measure;
My devotion is yours
And it will extend
Like my love, without limits,
For time without end.

GIFTS

I have the love and happiness for which I've always yearned,
I have the gifts of joy and peace that never can be earned;
I have a bank account of love, and wealthy in affection,
I have an indissoluble and deep soul connection;
I have a wealthy empire of truth and of trust,
A loving companionship impervious to rust;
Support, concern, and care are mine that never will decay,
Kindness and desire that time will never wear away;
I have a mint of partnership and fortune of content,
Kisses and embraces that are surely Heaven sent;
I have a union and devotion rare and seldom known,
That makes me feel a princess on a great, majestic throne;
I have all the priceless gifts that money cannot buy,
I have the love I've always hoped for, oh, how rich am I.

THOSE WE
HAVE LOVED

Those we've loved aren't lost to us
But hidden from our sight,
Awaiting us with loving hearts
When we reunite.

As when the storm has passed the raindrops
Vanish in the sun,
When cares of life have ceased, into
Your open arms I'll run.

My grieving heart, which lately wore
The gray shroud of sorrow,
Shall exchange it for the bright
Promise of tomorrow.

THE SOUL THAT LIVES WITHIN

Not with the body do I love you,
Which, with death, I leave behind,
But with the soul that lives within,
But with the spirit and the mind,
For many bodies have I worn
Upon the stage of centuries,
In many roles have I been clothed,
But I am yours eternally;
I've been so many faces, races,
Faiths, and nationalities,
But in whatever form expressed,
I'm all, yet I am none of these,
For, naked, I'm the soul inside,
Who, locked with you, in endless love,
Has found the one I'll journey with
Forevermore, in Heaven above.

FOREVER

I fall to my knees and cherish you
All of the days that are mine,
My love I give all the days I live
To you 'till the end of time.

I am yours forever and yours alone,
Nor other do I desire,
I will wait for you 'till my life is through,
For my love is yours entire.

TO MY BELOVED

Fairytale love that lives in a fable,
Commemorated in art,
That lives in the fame of Shakespeare's pen
Or the secret recess of the heart.

Rarest of gems that men pursue
For which they die or live,
Elusive love that lasts forever
To one another we give.

FOREVER YOURS

As upon an ageless script
Within the sanctum of the night
Upon the unseen scroll of time
This heart's testament I write.

I love you now, I loved you then,
Forever, past the grasp of time,
Witnessed in the sight of God
My love is yours, your love is mine.

THE RESURRECTION

Say that you will meet me tonight
In the kingdom of dream,
Let your arms encompass me
Although they are unseen,
For then the sorrow in my heart
Shall swift be turned to joy,
And kisses shall be mine once more
That time cannot destroy;
Let me clasp you, I who died, too,
When your soul took flight,
Oh, meet me there and I will live
Again tomorrow night.

THE FORTRESS

Here is a building of strong foundation;
I give you a fortress of structure worthy
Whose walls are solid, whose beams are sure,
Whose grounding level and ceiling sturdy
That will not fail in quake or trouble,
That will not fall with winds of years,
And if you'll dwell within this stronghold
You shall have no cause for fears;
Its architecture is a promise,
Word's devotion is its casting,
Of a sound construction bound
With vow of love, everlasting.

LOVE

It cannot be counted in watts or degrees,
In centimeters or grams,
It cannot be measured in mass or in force,
Its amount no scale commands;
It has no height, no depth, no size,
No substance of its own,
And only within its effect
Is its nature known;
It has no life, it has no form,
And yet is life's essence,
And, though unperceived, worlds
Are changed by its presence;
It has no bounds, it can't be seen,
Yet may be without end,
Freely given or received,
No man can buy or spend;
Not tasted, touched in any way
Known unto the sense,
It seems like nothing, yet no thing
Was ever so immense.

THE LION'S DEN

Not with a cautious heart half-warm
Do I discover your lips,
But with the consuming fire of
A full-emblazoned kiss.

Not with a tepid soul will I
Come to embrace you again,
But charge bold as Daniel did
Into the lion's den.

TEACH ME

Teach me not to feel
If you care not for me,
If your hours do not ache
As mine, relentlessly;
Teach me not to love
If ever we must part
And make me like the man of tin
Who doesn't have a heart;
If you long not for me,
As I for you do,
If you do not desire me always,
Love, as I do you,
Make me like the scarecrow,
Without a heart to die,
Make me like the shadow,
That never learned to cry.

THE ROAD

Before us there unfolds a road
Toward eternity;
The past remote, the future distant
Aren't ours to see;
From a puzzle we awake
And to a mystery go,
While guessing at a plan and purpose
We shall never know,
Until at last our lives diminish
As an echo dies,
Or as the ripples vanish on a pond,
Before our eyes.

THE REQUEST

I beg you, dear, my darling,
To be mine
Until we've spent our share
Of earthly time
And through the hourglass spilling
Sand has run,
Our journey to the great
Unknown begun,
And Heaven witnessing
My love for you,
Proclaims it's never seen
A love so true.

Λ THOUSAND LIVES

When I hear the silence of the end,
When I see the finish of my life,
When the works I've found to do our done,
When the lamp burns, but a feeble light,
Then will I reflect back into time,
The shadows that were once the friends I knew,
The memories I forged out of my life,
The dreams that were the deeds I chose to do,
And when I count the things I held most dear,
How rare is that one perfect love that's true,
And if I had a thousand lives to live
I would choose to live them all with you.

TOO SOON WE DIE

We die too soon, too soon the flower's
Fallen from the stem,
With too much haste the gold-crowned daisy
Yields her diadem,
To swift does night usurp the throne
Of sun within the sky,
Too rapidly our lives recede
As waters surging by,
So come and let us live today
And press your lips to mine,
Envelop me within your arms
And let our hearts combine,
Then though we can't reclaim the past,
Let's live in such a way
That we defy the dark
Oblivion of yesterday
And with our joy and love and laughter
Cast asunder sorrow,
With today eclipse the gray
Enigma of tomorrow.

THE PHANTOM LOVER

Betwixt the hours of dusk and dawn
Within the stillness of the night
You came to me so silently,
Enveloping me tight;

With gossamer arms you weaved me round,
And wafting a transparent kiss,
Contented me most thoroughly
With a phantom bliss.

BEFORE THE THRONE OF GOD

I will give all I have in life
To have you back again,
I will declare my love for you
Before this world of men,
Upon the highways, in the towns,
Wherever I may trod,
Upon my knees I'll ask for you
Before the throne of God.

TO PART NO MORE

No flesh obscures my feelings now
And you may read them like a book,
No heavy tongue lends awkward words,
For downward into my heart you look
And plainly see my love for you,
Revealed unto your spirit's eye,
And I shall join you where you are
To part no more, the day I die.

ALWAYS

The wide reaches of the world
Are made of atoms small
And the reservoir of sea
Of drops is formed withal;
The universe, so vast in size,
Is shaped in steps of miles,
And a count of photon coins
The sun's wealth compiles.

The commerce of the golden sand
Is meted out in grains
And forever, measured out,
Is only made of days,
And I shall love you, ever true,
In increments of days,
Never resting 'till I reach
The total of always.

DO NOT REND ME

Do not rend me with your eyes,
I cannot bear their teasing,
Nor in shyness cast them down
Whose laughter is so pleasing.

Do not sear me with their flame,
Who can't withstand their fire,
Nor give me too much space for hope,
Lest losing, I expire.

Do not pierce me with their tears,
Lest I die with their pain,
Nor remove them too far from
The heart that they sustain.

THE PROPRIETOR
OF MY HEART

You are brilliance enthroned in beauty
Inspiring awe
And unto the world of love
A natural law.

You are Aurora's rainbow,
The light that illumines the sky,
You are the wings of Mercury's feet
On which my fancies fly.

You are the wielder of Cupid's
Unerring dart,
You are the sole proprietor
Of my heart.

YOU

You were more than the sum of the wind and the sun
And the flowers and the blue of the sky,
You were far above the summer wind's love
For the dance of the clouds on high,
For you were the morning of April's dawning
And I found the sun in your eyes;
How could I know when we met it would show
You were summer's light in disguise,
And how could I tell before I knew well
The power you wielded that day,
For with feelings started, when you departed,
With you my heart went away.

MEASURES

How long is long? It's of a measure
Known subjectively,
For the ancient stars suppose
A thousand years are brief,
But from my perspective I
See it differently,
A second's time away from you
Defines eternity.

How far is far? It's of a distance
Open to debate,
For the sun feels a star
Is not so far away,
But from my point of view
A span gives alarms
Any time you're farther than
The compass of my arms.

How great is great? It's of a size
Figured by the heart,
For the moon lifts the tide
And never feels a smart,
But the sprawling universe
Is really not so much
When my love for you becomes
The rule by which I judge.

BOUNDARIES

How great is the love I have for you?
My love is vast and great as the sum
Of atoms that fill the universe through.

What limit can be in my love descried?
My love is much as the increments
Into which an inch we can divide.

When may my love's end you detect?
My love will endure until the time
Two lines in parallel intersect.

What height does my desire reach?
Its measure is great as the force two quarks
Must feel, attracting each to each.

When will the light of my love die?
When cause postdates effect, when matter
Can be destroyed, when truth can lie.

THE SECRET RENDEZVOUS

Place a phantom kiss upon my lips,
Enfold me in your energy embrace,
Caress me with electric fingertips,
Surprise me with a vision of your face;

Touch me with the substance of your soul,
So intimate that we combine and blend,
No portion of your spirit power withhold,
A love eternal, that beholds no end.

No place, no time, no manner wrong to meet,
No limit does our tender passion know,
For every tryst we have remains discreet,
Encounters we enjoy will never show.

Although no eyes our courtly romance see,
Your presence is reality to me,
Your ghostly amours from inquiry free,
Unhidden, woo me surreptitiously.

Who dares to say that ghosts do not exist
When our meetings fill me with such bliss;
Invisible to human eyes, we two,
Unseen, conduct our secret rendezvous.

THE LEAVETAKING

A tree is made of many parts,
Of branch, of leaf, of root, of bloom,
And each contributes to the total
Like the fibers on a loom;
The leaf is made to capture sun,
The root to take up nourishment,
The bloom is formed to pollinate,
The branch connects like ligament;
None can stand complete alone
But needs the others to survive,
As when I think of life without you
How, I ask, am I to thrive?
For you are heart unto my heart,
And you are life unto my soul,
Without you I'm a parted branch,
A severed bloom, and no more whole.

COME SAIL WITH ME

Come sail with me and be my love
And we will all the oceans rove
That wander far from shore to shore,
And all their cays and coves explore.

The shrouds shall make our lullaby,
The trees shall woo us with their sigh,
And, rocked to sleep by wind and wave,
We'll dream, embraced, in our enclave.

And I will make you beds of stars,
Our cloak the breeze, beneath the spars,
With nectar of the ocean spray,
Perfume from flowers of the bay,

The sun shall warm you with her light,
The moon shall guide our course at night,
And while Selene casts her charms,
We'll lie in one another's arms.

And if our hearts combine as one
We'll chart a reckoning, chase the sun,
And with our roof the heaven above,
Come sail with me and be my love.

CAPTOR OF
YOUR HEART

If I could be a countess
With a count to claim as mine,
A sovereign or a duchess
Of a duchy, I'd decline,
If I could be a conqueror
And make the world my own
Or be a mighty monarch
And sit upon a throne,
If I could be an empress
And wear an ermine gown
A lady or a queen,
I would turn these titles down,
Princess or her highness
Could never placate me;
The captor of your heart
Is all I care to be.

WHAT ARE THESE WORDS?

What are these words you'll never hear?
What is the smile you'll never see?
And if they will never hold you tight,
What are these arms worth to me?

What are possessions, degrees and fame,
All of the money that I could earn,
No more than a vain and foolish game
That never could buy your return.

What are my days if without you,
What are the years wasted alone,
What is this thing called the future,
Cold and dead and lifeless as stone.

I WANT TO LOOK UPON THOSE EYES

I want to look upon those eyes
Whose blue is locked within my mind,
Where, like a treasure, they remain
Secure from all who hope to find,
I want to place my head upon
The shoulder, where, from all the world's
Misfortunes I am kept, and safe
From all its darts and arrows hurled,
I want to rest within those arms
Where I'll at last discover peace,
In which I'll cast all tears away,
From which I'll never seek release.

MY ALL

When everything I have is gone,
Yet you are my everything,
For there's no thing that I desire
Beyond the life and joy you bring;
I do not love the job you have,
I do not covet any wealth,
I care no whit what you possess,
But love you only for yourself;
Of all I am and all I have,
However great, however small,
There's nothing that I will not give
To be with you, my all.

IF YOU POSSESSED

If you possessed a fortune's wealth
Or counted nothing as your own,
If your friends were numberless
Or if you sat sad nights alone,
If you felt unloved or if
You looked on lost years with regret,
If you lacked a shirt to wear
Or lived in excess, or in debt,
If you wore the weight of age
Or met the years unscathed and strong,
If your days were but a few
Or if your time on earth was long,
If you shared the world's success
Or disappointments were your part,
With nothing, yet you are my all,
The one who won and holds my heart,
For you are more than all this world,
Forevermore my everything,
All I ever hoped and dreamed,
My hero, knight, my prince and king,
And, proud to be the one beside you,
All upon the earth I'd tell
About the luckiest woman alive
Who wants you, whom you want as well.

THE WEDDING

Wake up, you songbirds, sing aloud,
And earth, go preen, in gown of Spring,
Shine sun, as you have never shown
For there awaits a gathering;
Soon now, the long-desired time,
When grief shall be a shadow past,
And joy shall take the place of pain
For two whose happiness will last,
And there within that better world
We'll find each other once again,
A wedding of two hearts which long
Before this moment should have been,
And with new life and blessings crowned
And with contentment that endures,
How joyously I will be gathered
To your breast, forever yours.

IF

If from the sky the sun should stray
To leave the world in endless night
Then you should be my only sun
And I'd not lack for warmth and light,
Or if the moon should disappear
Some night, I'd never lose my way,
For, blackest night, beholding you,
Transforms itself to brightest day;
If all the world contains should vanish,
Yet how small would be the cost
If you remain with me, my love,
For I would never feel their loss,
But if your life is taken, I
Should count as suffering every breath
And since your life is one with mine
For loss of you I'd welcome death.

THE LETTER

Dear love, in beholding all
The visions of the fleeting show
That form the record of my life,
Observing faces come and go
As from the window of a train,
The scenes appear and flicker by;
In hours of the heart how brief
The time we live before we die,
And though in hours of the clock
It seems that youth will never pass,
Why, even our imperfect eyes
Can see no mortal thing can last;
Though we stand stalwart like the sun
Does in the zenith of her day,
Yet like the sun in our own dusk
Our lives decline and fade away,
And when I ponder all of this,
How limited a time is mine,
How small the part I have to play
Within this infinite design,
Then I'm reminded that of all
That I could have or I could do
That nothing's worth as much to me
As having and as loving you.

DISCOVERIES

I know the way they must have felt,
The naturalist, Von Leeuwenhoek,
Who found a world unknown to man
Beneath his probing microscope,
And wayfaring Columbus who
Set sail with his courageous band,
Defying ocean's rage and wrath
To set afoot on virgin land,
Or brave Cortez, conquistador,
Who, new horizons to explore,
Atop a peak in Darien
Beheld the blue Pacific shore,
Or Galileo, who with scope
Affixed upon the firmament,
Beheld the shining Milky Way
With mingled awe and wonderment,
For worlds that I had never known
Unfolded, new, before my sight
When there within your eyes I found
The one true love of my life.

COMPARED WITH YOU

I've seen the things this world can give,
The hollow titles, passing fame,
I've seen the idols of the past
So worshipped once, forgotten names;
I've seen its wealth, its foolish pride
That beckon man, a pretty lie
For which they strive throughout their lives,
Attain but for a space, and die;
I've seen the lovely face of youth,
The form and shape that cannot last
But fade like every beauteous thing
Into the darkness of the past;
I've seen the best that men possess
And weighed the things that men accrue,
But all that life can offer me
Is nothing when compared with you.

THE ABDUCTION

How precious you are as a gem-rich mine
Laden in emerald or diamond design,
How infinite, too, as the stars at night
Receding, endless, before our sight;
I await the day my aching dreams
Transform as shifting, cloud-form scenes
And what the darkness of distance conceals
The bright and breathless day reveals,
For swift as an actor dons a mask
Into my arms you'll sweep at last,
With a kiss that is, itself, day
To the night of the season you spent away,
A kiss that brushed my lips and stole
To the very boundaries of my soul;
Our hearts will beat, attuned in time,
As the coupled words of a bard's rhyme,
You'll touch me softly, we'll unite,
Become my vision and my light,
I'll press you to me, we'll combine
And all the wealth of the world is mine,
In your eye's paths I'll stray,
And heaven and earth shall vanish away.

DELICATE
THINGS ONLY

Delicate things only belong
With thoughts of you,
Thunder is wrong,
Although what I feel
Sometimes is like
Thunder's peal;
Roses and daffodils might describe
What's blooming inside,
Though whitecaps dancing
Lightly over the waves
Portrays when you're near
How my heart behaves.

THE STRONGHOLD

I thought to build for my defense
A stately fortress residence
As of a prince in feudal times
And so rest safe in its confines,
With buttress for its soaring towers,
And moat to defy the mightiest powers,
Turrets peaking high with pride,
Artillery at every side,
I stationed guards at every wall
And set a lookout over all
This great and glorious place to dwell,
This garrisoned stronghold nonpareil,
That lives no enemy to defeat;
Yet but a chink undoes the wall,
My matchless fortress starts to fall;
One lovely smile has stolen in,
Two lovely eyes all contests win:
Then conquer me, for you are best,
Abash me, I do not protest.

THIS DUSTY EMPIRE

You have not loved, nor heard, nor seen,
Nor governed, but as a sovereign of dream;
You have not hearing, sense or sight
To draw a new world from devouring night
If you have not loved; but discover love
And with its power you will command
All paradise that a man may demand
And reign as one who is deified,
But if I must lack you at my side
I shall scorn its favors and abide,
Softly close the gates of my heart,
Its mansions abandoning to the dark,
And sleep until time shall wear away
This dusty empire compounded of clay.

THE CONSPIRACY

Your eyes were never innocent,
Your smile must share the blame,
Although your tender words were sweet
They're guilty all the same;
Your gentle touch I loved so much
Was nonetheless at fault,
Not to mention your embrace,
A conquering assault,
For cheek and lip and shining hair
Each assumed a part
To overthrow my judgment
And conspired to steal my heart.

EMPTY ARMS

I tell of you, who took my heart,
And vanquished it complete,
Who conquered every thought and brought
Resistance to defeat.

I tell of you who brought me to
Submission with your charms,
And in return for this indenture
Filled my empty arms.

THE TOUCH OF YOUR HAND

The snow like a blanket of white down
Overspreads the darkened ground,
Wintering all the browns in white,
Like a man turned ancient overnight,
While the wind shaves through the warmest coats
And pipes through the door her tuneless notes,
And I sit comfortably inside,
In the warmth of the home where I reside,
And am content without a fire,
Since your eyes have warmed me with desire,
And have no need for a glass of wine,
When I feel the touch of your hand in mine.

THE FALL

Your arms closed around me
And I bid farewell
To the watchman who had kept my heart
And my defenses fell;

And then when you had drawn me close
I felt the touch of fate
But little did I care that my
Protest had come too late;

The moment that became a kiss
Marked the fateful start
Of my surrender as I bid
You welcome in my heart.

SLEEPER

Sleeper, wherefore do you sleep
This sleep so sound, so still and deep,
Was it a draught of river Lethe
That brought this dreamless sleep as death,
Or did your drowsy slumber fall
When you were charmed by night bird's call?
Did Morpheus in wild disguise
Enchant your heavy-lidded eyes?
Pray, how came you to be this way,
Immune to early morning's ray,
Or is it that in realms of sleep
Your arms about her you may keep
And that you wish no more to wake
But dream forever for her sake.

THE PRISONER

When, beautiful love, into your eyes
I looked, and when I first beheld your face,
When you opened up your heart to me,
Admitting me to your most secret place,
It was as though a passage opened wide,
And entering in, behind me closed the door,
While I had left behind me yesterday
And through its portal could return no more,
For, touching you, a mighty wind that I
Could not resist swept my heart away,
And, loving you, a strong, relentless tide
Drew my thoughts to you, where still they stay;
Confined within a prison beautiful
And from all desire for others free,
I am bound with ties of love to you
And in them comprehend true liberty.

THE SEAS OF NEVERMORE

Where are the self-important men,
Where the heroes of yesteryear,
Who took the helm of the world a while,
Then left to another the course to steer,
Where are the faces I recall,
The names I carry within my heart,
Whose warmth I felt in a touch, a smile,
Before they were summoned to depart?
Where is the eye whose light I knew
That shown, like a beacon unto me,
But now is at rest, forever closed,
As a ghost within my memory?
As we await within the dark
Our call, alone upon the shore,
They've made the voyage everlasting
On the seas of nevermore.

YOU AND I ALONE

When your eyes discover mine,
When our lips combine as one
The world, it seems, is born anew
And life has just begun,
For history is a fable dim,
The future but a fragile dream,
And all about me are but phantoms
And not what they seem;
You and I alone exist,
The world's adventures fade away
Within the mist we name tomorrow
Or its shadow, yesterday.

THE STRUCTURE
SLEEPS IN DUST

The structure sleeps in dust
With hollow, empty halls
Where no footsteps echo off
The mute, forgetting walls,
The walk grows up in grass
And spiders spin their webs
On doors no longer opened
While time discreetly ebbs,
Offices are darkened,
Their tenants gone away,
While all is turned to silence
Save the wind's mournful lay.
Vacant corridors
As images in mirrors
Recede into the distance
Where no figure e'er appears,
Here all the works of man
Have come unto their end
And in a faceless, nameless past
They wordlessly descend.

THE GEMSTONE LIFE

To mine the gemstone life,
To gather its hidden grace
Demands four eyes, yours and mine,
To discover the secret place.

Though I have but two to guide me,
Should I chance upon the treasure,
While you stand behind as I make the find
Will you wish we had ventured together?

HAVING YOU

Some men conspire as they desire
To gain what they pursue,
And having made a million dollars
Then desire two;

Some men don't stop before the top
And having won acclaim,
Aspire to objectives new
And greater heights of fame;

Though without cease, I once sought peace,
Its face I never knew,
But I consent that I'm content
Forever, having you.

ALL I DESIRE

I desire no thing for having
All that I desire
And am content, nor is there ought
I purpose to acquire,
For, having you, I have the world
And do not wish for more,
For I have now the truth I dreamed
And ever waited for.

MORE FAIR

More fair than portraits from the master's brush,
More lovely is your face
Then any masterpiece that's made
Of human loveliness and grace,

More beautiful than poets' lines,
More wondrous is your smile
Than all that ever has been said
Of ornament and style.

More music lies within your voice
Than symphony or song,
A melody I've dreamed to hear
A lonely life time long.

THIS PRISON

When once I knew your kiss
And to you closely pressed,
When your arms 'compassed me
And I lay on your breast,
When in your arms enfolded
As shadows 'round the night
Until the dawn's unveiling
We lay embracing tight;

Since I have known your presence
To now be cleaved apart
Is like a grief most potent
Piercing through my heart,
And sundered from your touch,
No other one can mend
This prison without walls,
This torment without end.

FORCES

Streams of liquid fire,
Shooting frothy spumes
Arise from deep
Subterranean sleep
Within their silent tombs.
Frenzied, dueling winds
Of dervish-whirling storms
When indiscreet
Air masses meet
Are all a-sudden born.
From out its burning forge
Spews fire from the sun,
Whose heat and light
The skies ignite
With fusing hydrogen.
A supernova bright,
A massive star that dies,
As dynamite
Within the night
Explodes throughout the skies.
My love, so like their force,
Though some can calculate
And can assess,
Seems limitless
And infinitely great.

FREE TIME

Free time, yes, free time to spare,
Free time to read, to write, to do,
Free time to watch the world go by,
To sit and wish I were with you.

Free time to spend whatever way,
To dance, to play the notes of song,
To paint or go out for a drive,
Free time to think of you and long.

Free time to go where my heart leads,
Free time, imposter's rude deceit,
To watch the clock upon the wall
And count the hours 'till next we meet.

HOW WILL A FOOL PAY?

How will a fool pay for a second chance
With eyes of tears, with nights that see no sleep,
With ache, regret, remorse, but no relief,
With days of pain that seem without an end,
A heart that breaks which none can ever mend,
With eyes that, ceaseless, view a past mistake
And heart that would do all to but reshape,
With useless days and longing, lonely nights
And feelings that no other can requite,
With lonely arms that wait until the day
That grief and time can all be swept away,
With pain that cuts my heart as would a knife,
With my all, my labor, and my life,
For I'd give all, that moment to relive,
And then regret I had no more to give.

Λ CRESCENDO OF THE SUN

I will build around me
A crescendo of the sun
And when discordant notes assail
My tune will overcome.

I'll establish all about
A shield of vibrant light
And when the shadows make their siege
I'll banish them from sight.

THE COMPASS

Many courses are set
And many paths are taken,
Many harbors are called home
And many journeys forsaken.

Many ways are lost
And many dreams fail,
Many alleys prove blind
And many visions pale.

But I've a compass true,
A guide that cannot err,
A destination my heart has set,
And you'll be waiting there.

FOR LOVE OF YOU

Of stars the night sky I would sweep
To pave a pathway for your feet,
The shower's rainbow would I rob,
A lucky charm for you to keep,
The flowers would I gather fresh
To fill the softness of your bed,
The very sun would I ensnare
To shine wherever you should tread,
The heavens and the earth would I
Secure within a pretty bow,
Present and place before your feet
That you, without a doubt, should know
I love you so, and I would do
This and more, for love of you.

NO MORE THE SAME

I loved the way the bud-scents blew
Along a rural lane
Before the wind, but you are gone
And they're no more the same.

I loved the way the wave-cliffs rose
From out the heaving main
Behind the swell, but you are gone
And they're no more the same.

I loved the way the dawn was born
Upon a rose-red stain
Of vaulted heights, but you are gone
And they're no more the same.

I loved the way the sun's ray
Reposed on virgin shore
Of sand-white bay, but you are gone
And they're the same no more.

UNMEASURED WEALTH

My raiment may be bare of thread,
The years betray I'm growing old,
But when I look into your eyes
I discover wealth untold.

Though I grow poor and lame and halt,
Endure disintegrating health,
Destitute of fortune's meed,
I have in you unmeasured wealth.

THE OLD HOUSE

The old house stands
Stamped with decay,
Bereft of all
That time has swept away;
The old pump house
With its roof of tin,
The red-roofed barn
With floor caving in.
The bright sun porch
With morning birds beside,
The elk-crowned hearth
That once bespoke pride,
The old piano rolls
And oval photographs,
An attic filled with boxes
Of outmoded hats,
The old swinging door,
The tarpaper walk,
The whippoorwills and crickets
In their nightly talk,
Home of my youth,
When you have passed away,
Part of you will be with me
To my dying day.

I WANT TO LIVE

I don't want to write, I want to live,
To hold you, love you for a space as mine,
Possess you if but for a moment's measure
Before we vanish in the tide of time.

I don't want to place our names in poems,
Insuring them an immortality,
For while I may look into your eyes
I have no thought for posterity.

My letters I shall translate into kisses,
With you the parchment on which I shall write,
My words shall be for you alone to see
Before our eyes are closed in endless night.

When the world forgets you and me
And passes us as if we'd never been
The darkness into which we cannot see
Shall claim us, let us live for now, not then.

In this little chapter that is life
With a void beyond and before,
Come into my arms and share this love
Now, before the closing of the door.

THE VISION

Thou walkest sunbeams.
Consist of air,
A mount your heart,
Nocturnal jasmine in your hair.

Showers are your radiant smiles
Drawn from the fathoms of a sea,
A glade of flowers in your touch
Plucked from the forest Mystery,
That makest hand and heart confess
Your most perfect, perfect loveliness.

THE INNER LOVE

The flower's but a garment like a cloth
And in its depth the nectar is confined,
The jewel's resplendence, so admired of men,
Is hidden in the framework of the mine,
The treasure's stored within the schooner's hold,
The pearl's sequestered in the oyster's shell,
The story lies submerged within its book,
And DNA lies deep within its cell,
So man within a mortal scaffold dwells,
That's subject to the ravages of time,
But even through this tattered suit, the love
We wear within will never fail to shine.

TO THE NAYSAYERS

They say a rainbow's end
May never be attained
And that its treasure trove
No mortal ever gained,
But I did not believe
The words they spread around
And so I took that rainbow
And wear it as a crown.

They said there was a land
That lived within the mind,
A perfect paradise
No man could ever find,
But I did not accept
The tales that they tell
And now that paradise is
The kingdom where I dwell.

The phoenix that arose
From ashes' death to live
They say did not exist
As more than but a myth,
But strange as it may seem
From hope that was oppressed
That phoenix rose to give me life
And sings within my breast.

THE SHIP

There a golden galleon sits
With banner streaming, masts set proud,
Sails stretched, and rigging strained,
Sheeted in, with taut-locked shroud,
And rudder set, she steers a course
The stars alone, above her, know
And her bold prow that parts the wave
Follows where the currents go,
But never does she make her port
Though greater ship no sailor knew
For on my mantelpiece she sits
And dreams of travel, as I do.

PARADISE

Not to the north do I live
With bearded trees with snow-girt thighs
That lend the winter winds their cries,
Nor south, in the land whose perennial spy
Glances down on the land with a feverish eye,
Nor east, where the green is less of the land
Than the green of the outstretched merchant's hand,
Nor with the wayfarers of the west,
Home of the homeless, where the restless rest,
No, I make my home in the clime of his eyes,
In a province of the heart,
In a state of the mind
Called Paradise.

THE CALCULATION

I'd have as many as words in print,
As coins issued from the mint,
As all that's sweet or salt or swill,
As all the court's brocade or frill,
A sum of drops to make a flood
Of all the saintly martyrs' blood,
Enough to fill the skies and seas,
Or taxes the federal treasury,
As many as men have lived and died,
As women who over those men have cried,
As money lost or gained or spent,
Much as landlords exact in rent,
As praises that 'scape the preacher's mouth,
As many as roads as travel south;
Then I'll have totaled nine billion
Nine hundred ninety-two,
And that's one short of the kisses
I should modestly hope of you.

PUZZLE'S PIECE

I've searched the scented country glades
Composed of sun and summer's shades,
And wandered fertile summer's fields
That still no long-sought answer yield,
In solitude I've sought the key
And searched in crowd and company,
I've traveled o'er the oceans far
And asked the mute, indifferent stars,
But nowhere found the missing piece
That I've pursued so without cease,
And I've meandered sunny slopes
While weary with unanswered hopes
And followed city street and town
But never the solution found
To cover up this empty place,
This lonely void I can't erase,
This puzzle's piece I'm seeking still,
The place that you alone can fill.

TO BE A KING

I don't long to be a king
With crowds bowed down before me,
I don't long to act a play
For legions who adore me,
I don't long to harbor wealth
And call the world my own,
For I have all the wealth I need
Possessing you alone,
You've made me happiest of men,
If I do this for you,
Then I've done what I desire
And my labor's through,
And since you've said that you'll be mine,
If I can be your own,
I would not exchange this for
A kingdom or throne.

I WILL WAIT FOR YOU

Until the snows descend,
The dark storm is at hand,
Until the lightning strikes
And winds defile the land,
Until the thund'rous clouds
Clamor through the sky
And the dueling crosswinds
Cause the trees to cry,
Until the deepening shadows
Draw the sheath of night
Across the bier of barren earth
And the lifeless blight
Called death arrives, declaring
My days of life are through
Until that time, wait for me,
As for you I do,
Wait for me, wait for me,
I will wait for you.

WORDS

Words, a wondrous, bewitching elixir,
Words, a magic, fantastical web,
Words, a mental motion picture,
Images that flow and ebb,
Words to charm or to delight
Shielding darkness, yielding light,
Words that move and words that thrill,
That drive men's hearts to love or kill,
Words that win and words that woo,
But what are words if they're untrue,
A quaint mirage made of air,
A winding path that leads nowhere,
A useless note no one can spend
That yields a worthless dividend,
So shrive my words and sift them through,
Test their worth in fire and flue
For their strength and value hold,
Coined in trust and backed in gold,
Weigh their promise, try their proof,
In word and deed my love is truth;
While often words are left undone,
You'll find my oath and act are one.

THE AWAKENING

Is it the world that's changed, or is it my sight?
Why are the nights more vivid, the days more bright?

How should it be that the commonest things beguile?
Or is it just that they wear my interior smile?

What are these feelings that erstwhile evaded me
As though I had never before been able to see?

Are they a mirror of the feelings you stirred inside,
Or is it perhaps that before I was half alive?

THE HIBERNATION

My earth, my sky, my moon, my sun,
My very heaven, if there be one,
My joy, my happiness, my wealth,
Whom I love more than life itself,
Before I knew there was a you,
How did I live, what did I do;
No, never mind, for that's the past,
The best is here, save best for last,
The moment that I share with you
I've waited for my lifetime through,
For when I look upon your face
The world becomes a different place
And when our hands and hearts combine
My life is new, the world is mine,
But when you must depart from me
You fill my thoughts continually;
'Till you return, my heart shall wait,
Forsaking life to hibernate.

FORGOTTEN NAMES

Beyond the earth's convex curve the sun
Waning slowly, lonely, swiftly sinks,
As fast as man's flagging lifetime fades
In the space of time an eyelid blinks,
From youth to age and to debility,
He surges on from peak into decline,
And seldom learns to know humility
Before he's called from labors to resign,
And then unto a lonely place, the grave,
A quiet home to morbid flesh and bone,
Go pauper, beggar, emperor, and slave
From gutter, cottage, palace, shack, and throne,
And there, deployed in close proximity,
From separate stations, many tiers in life,
They join the ranks of anonymity,
Daughter, son and husband, cousin, wife,
For no longer mentioned, thought of, known,
Remembered, in the very briefest time
It shall be as though they never lived,
Forgotten names, as yours will be and mine.

TO A DETECTIVE

Tell me, sage investigator,
When you look within my mind
Of the nature of the substance
Which therein you chance to find,

Or if you should yet further delve
And sound the fathoms of my heart,
What dwells therein for you to find
When you attain the deepest part?

Or if you peer within my eyes
To see the image hid therein,
What thing shall be sequestered there
When my eyes' farthest reach you win?

Oh, shrewd detective, you shall pry
From heart, from eye, the hidden wealth
To find behind my every door
The very likeness of yourself.

CH3'S LOVE
SONG FOR CL2

When we touched my balance was overcome;
You disrupted my equilibrium;
When I came into your energy field
I had no other recourse but to yield;
It's trite to say we were made for each other,
But we've an attraction, one for another,
That you might be pleased to call chemistry
That pulls me to you and draws you to me;
It's so hard to tolerate being alone
Since you entered my electrophilic zone;
If we were to find the right orientation
We might develop a spatial relation,
Your geometry has made me grow fond
And I've such an intense desire to bond,
Let's bridge our threshold of activation,
Together we'd make the perfect equation,
But say we can resonate together,
There could be no greater earthly pleasure;
If each of us were willing to share
We'd make an ideal electron pair,
Why, you could give and I would take,
What sweet resonance we would make,
'Twould take a strong rival to pull us apart,
We were meant to unite, right from the start.

CHANGE

Is nothing now constant but change itself?
For protons are bound even to decay
And matter transforms into energy
While neither within its own state will stay;
Chaos, a fundamental law,
Says nature to randomness now must yield,
And since as observers we alter fact,
No more does a particle's fate seem sealed,
And out of all this uncertainty
Where everything seems but subject to change,
I'll love you forever, whatever that means,
But please don't insist I explain.

WORLD OF
THE IDEAL

Can I live with you in your world of ideas?
Is there room enough for two?
I'm sure that Hegel and Hume won't mind
If I spend some time with you,
For on reflections we shall dine
And on conjectures think,
While thoughts shall be our draught of wine,
Ideas our meat and drink,
For Hume's design will we discuss
And Mill's utility,
With Locke's empiricism, test
Our minds' ability.
The noumina of Kant will we
Submit for speculation,
To Aristotle's logic we will
Turn our rumination,
No arguments will we sustain
Save in philosophy,
But spend our days' and nights' repose
In perfect harmony,
And we shall ponder Plato's theory,
Prove his tenets real,
And live, a perfect couple, in
Our world of the ideal.

THIS VOYAGE

This voyage long and arduous I make
Upon the dark and looming seas alone,
Without a map or chart to undertake
This journey, far from harbor, port, or home;
No compass have I, save the course of trust,
No courage but for faith to comfort me,
No friendly star to save me from the thrusts,
Assaults, and sieges of the angry sea,
No co-pilot have I to set my course,
To guide my craft and spare me short relief,
No refuge from the storm and no resource
Apart from will, conviction, and belief,
For hope is all I have in my endeavor
Of promise that my path will lead to you,
And that, one day, we might spend life together,
Before my journey's reckoning is through.

FOR WHICH TO LIVE, FOR WHICH TO DIE

For our short lease and tenancy
Upon this satellite
Within the vast environs of
The universal night,
In looking on the stars that weave
The fabric of the sky,
I query, of what import is
A creature such as I,
So unremarkable within
Its framework and design,
Who labor but a day before
My summons to resign;
I wonder what the cause shall be
That justifies this life,
Or what might be the object that
Can dignify the fight,
For which to live, for which to die,
Endure adversity,
Within this world one worthy thing
Alone I've found to be
My reason to continue when
No other can I find,
To call your priceless love my own,
And know that you are mine.

THE WINDS OF TIME

From whence it is, we know not,
But it comes billowing, the wind,
Sweeping all from out its path;
It, like time, has always been.

The names of fame, like history's deeds,
Live, in time, but for a day
And then like silken spider's nets
In the storm, are washed away.

Truth and trust and words of man
Are fashioned but to fade and die,
And like the season's transient glory
Leave no traces, passing by.

For as a brisk wind casts about
At whim, the light and fragile feather,
So does time remove the years
And faces, lost forever.

No love at all

Will I tire of you when you tire,
When flesh concedes and tendons ail,
Will I forsake when pains assail?

Will you reject me when I fall,
When worldly cares become too much,
When I weaken and need a crutch?

Will I deny you when infirm,
And aches assault you without cease,
When abilities decrease?

Will you shun me when I weaken,
When I feel the hand of age,
When time has turned another page?

Will I abandon when you wear,
With sight less sharp and hand more weak,
When you're no longer at your peak?

Will you desert me when I fail,
If no longer strong and hail,
When my charms and beauties pale?

No, I do not think it so,
Nor would I forswear and go,
For one who would or one who can

Would love the flesh and not the man;
What kind of love, when hardships fall
Would withdraw — no love at all.

BORROWED ONLY

So difficult to be apart
With you held there and I held here,
Desiring you with all my heart,

A grief, each moment of the day,
Without you, so unsure, I fall,
But rise, with faith, resume my way.

But I am merely marking time,
And, lonely for you, if I err,
Forgive me that unwitting crime.

Whatever of works I find to do,
I'm borrowed only by this life,
Forever I belong to you.

I WANT TO CLAIM
YOU A CROWN

I want to claim you a crown,
A trophy to lay at your feet,
With Hercules' labors and victory's savors
And adversary's defeat.

I want to create you a song,
A music so haunting and sweet,
To lull the dread Sirens and charm the environs
When passion and melody meet.

I want to build you a city,
A city gleaming and bright,
With spires and choirs and melodious lyres
And steeples resplendent and white.

I want to give you the world
And share all its joys together,
But, failing of these, nothing else would so please
As to love you anon and forever.

THE PORTRAIT

You are the portrait
Rembrandt could not draw;
You are the lines
That failed Browning's pen;
You are the song
Debussy wished to hear,
The wonder never captured
In the finest arts of men,
The living soul of beauty
That I feel within my breast,
Where, in the substance of my heart
Your splendor is expressed,
For I have found the greatest beauty
That the world can give,
And in the threshold of your arms
I come to life and live.

WHEN I FIRST SAW YOU

When I first saw you, 'twas as though
The sun exploded in my eyes,
And who was I to bind that one
Who, timeless eons, lights the skies;

When I beheld you first, it seemed,
A mighty wave had covered me,
And who was I to quell the seas
That have roamed eternally;

When you first beguiled my sight
The heavens drew apart, immersing
Me within their jeweled light,
And who was I, but flesh and blood,
To withstand this stellar flood.

ANGUISH

You will always be to me
The unfinished work,
The unfulfilled hope,
The unrealized dream
That crumbled and broke,
A heart dashed to pieces,
Yet knowing pain,
Dreams that are gone,
And aches that remain
That cannot be relieved
But only confessed,
And the anguish that
Cannot be expressed.

MY LORD

In this dusk and shadowed realm
With Darkness' pilot at the helm
We suffer trouble, toil, and care
Amongst the burdens that we bear,
While justice falls before the sword;
Through faith alone we know our Lord;
Where love is always undermined,
But for faith, we stumble, blind,
But, at last, we trust there is
A better kingdom that is His,
Where trust and truth are not maligned
By power's lies and lust's design,
Where love and justice shall prevail
And no more fiery darts assail,
Where I'll find those things dear to me
Amongst a glorious company,
The finest things that man can know,
The highest things that Heaven bestow,
All things bright and pure and true,
And at the summit I shall see
My Lord, and love, and you.

BESIDE YOU

For whom I live,
For whom I dare to die,
For whom there is no price
I would not give,
Nor summit that I'd hesitate to try.

For whom I'd give my land,
My home, my hearth,
For whom I'd cast security away,
For whom I give the total of my heart,
For whom I give the number of my days.

For whom I give my pledge
Of faith forever,
To be a partner to my final breath,
For whom I wait until we are together,
And make my place beside you after death.

Λ WONDER

What makes his blue eyes unlike any others,
Commingled with the warmest of greens,
What makes his walk so distinct from the thousands
That my eyes encounter in everyday scenes?

What makes his smile seem one in a million,
What makes his demeanor stand out from the rest,
And what makes his favor that one in a billion,
All others forsaken, that I deem the best?

For what are we all but machines finely hewn,
And yet that machine has my heart torn asunder,
But what are we still, but machines finely tuned,
And yet, to my soul, still he is a wonder.

I REMEMBER

I remember a smile
As warm as any sun,
A mind that grew so close
We often thought as one,
A simple heartfelt word
That meant much more than gold,
And many special moments
That never can be told;
In quiet recollection
They pass before my mind,
And in the midst of efforts
They follow close behind,
For into one sparse room
You brought the world entire,
Love, wisdom, understanding,
Were its rich attire,
And though its poor adornments
Were meager and were few,
You filled it with a wealth
That princes never knew.

ETERNITY

With the fall of evening
The drowsy flowers withdraw
And sleep until the morning sun
Awakens with her call.

The sunshine warms the earth
And visits on each flower,
But must of duties be relieved
By the insistent shower.

But like the patient clock
That knows of no such rest,
Eternity shall find you hidden
Undisturbed within my breast.

SUSTENANCE

You are the sustenance of my love,
Which, like the life contained in the flower,
Folds its petals and withers within
Without the restoring caress of the shower.

You are the substance of my hope,
A flower that blooms with the kiss of the sun
And lifts her face to receive his love,
Or wilts without her beloved one.

TWIN STARS

Here by the water's brink I lie
On a moon-bright beach with a star-strewn sky
Whose beacons float in lazy light,
Lending kisses to the night,
That land upon the churning sea
And sparkle like a fantasy
On waves sculptured like confection,
Dancing under the wind's direction,
Which, then, streams across the land;
Such is the gentle touch of your hand.

The globe that glows within the night
Spreads moonlit tracks of phantom light
Upon the bosom of the sea,
Just as your words, imprints in me.

The meteor, so silent, glides,
In silver filaments, divides
The empty regions of the night
In rivulets of streaming light,
In shining furrows passing through
As thoughts of you, that pierce me through.

The cloud in garb of gossamer
Steals near the moon, embracing her,
And as the stars wink, sleepily,
You, like a cloud, close over me.

And then as sails, tightly furled,
We draw the curtain of the world,
Twin-stars, wed each to his lover,
Merge, and sink into one another.

THE SOUND OF OUR HEARTS

All is aglow in ethereal light
From the mist-frosted moon this eerie night;
Where errant star-beams chase in flight,
I move through the shadows of darkened night,
With a crisp-fresh breeze distracting my hair
And a curious potion in the air,
A heavy fragrance sedating the seas,
Distilled in the chalice of blossoming trees,
And the pebbles on shore like jewels inlaid,
A-glisten in tones of moonbeams waylaid;
Through murky diffusions of darkness I veer,
At last, through confusions of shades I draw near
To the sheltered glade encircled with trees
That appears as a shrine where ancient decrees
Were pronounced on a long past summer's night
And have long since died, a primeval rite;
Here, the wind in sleepy starts
Teases the leaves and then departs;
I take you into my arms as night
Enfolds us in vestments of shimmering light,
While the moon-witch withdraws to her mystical arts
And the sea is deafened with the sound of our hearts.

DREAMS

When I sleep I dream of creatures strange,
Of monsters and goblins,
Of stairways that creak,
Of odd relations and cats that speak,
Of moonlit seas,
And phantom ships,
But if I should dream,
I would rather these,
The shapes that fill
My head as I wake,
The thought of you that instantly brings
A thousand daffodils scattered with spring,
The fountain of laughter,
A breeze of sighs,
The colorful burst
Of a rainbow sky,
The music of words
That I love to hear,
In my heart, the sunrise
Of holding you near.

WONDERS

Four point five odd billion years
Have vanished since the world began,
Three hundred thousand years have superseded
Since the birth of man,
One hundred sixty nations make
Their home upon the planet earth
And on this globe five billion Homo
Sapiens subsist and work,
While cities by the thousands thrive
Where men in many millions dwell,
So looking at the figures it
Is hardly difficult to tell,
That I should not a gambler need
To read the odds confronting me;
No statistician would I seek
To see the probability,
That on the great expanse of time
We might sojourn to find each other,
Or traverse the universe
To spend our lives with one another;
With the years we could have lived
Our chance to meet we might have missed,
But you and I the odds defy;
Who says that wonders don't exist?

CONFLICTS

The forays of war wage in my heart,
The pierces of my conscience smart,
But the flesh has hurt my conscience more,
Though both are scathed in mortal war,
For wounded flesh cries out in pain
To know its hopes for triumph vain,
And conscience drops its head in shame
For flesh has made its virtues lame,
And neither plays a stronger part,
But both cause conflicts in my heart,
Which suffers more than either one
When the count of casualties is done.

WINTER

Look at you, winter, dressed in white,
A white frock to warm you at night,
A white habit, and white shoes,
A pair of snow white pantaloons,
A white hat and a white fur coat,
A star-bright necklace worthy of note,
A muffler of white, a soft white gown,
A bare body of white when you lie down.

LOVE AND NATURE

The tall tufts of meadow grass
Arch their backs like dancers,
The ash trees flash a silver code
To the singing wind's answer,
The reedy pool, deep and cool,
Is visited by the dragonfly,
The regal burrs with mossy heads
Repose in fragrant green beds
And spindly weeds with golden crowns
Court the buds in purple gowns;
I long to hold you to me here
In Nature's private hemisphere
And in my arms you'll descend
As Love and Nature choose to blend.

THE STARS THAT ARE YOUR EYES

The stars that are your eyes this night
Are artisans of my delight
And shine but that I might admire
Your hair's diffuse and brilliant fire,
Which gives unto the rose to speak
The hues that lie upon your cheek,
Which, mixed with sunlight from your smile,
And melodies your words compile,
With shadows that become your tears,
Distilled from dews throughout the years,
Combine as song-strains from afar,
So that all things about you are
A template unto Nature's art
And make enchantment of my heart.

ALL I DESIRE

When I have you, dear, next to me,
I've wealth and riches none can see;
Though I've no kingdom, crown or throne,
The world is mine, and mine alone,
And when I look within your eyes,
Though I have no court or guard to prize,
No castle and no heraldry,
I know that monarchs envy me,
For, having you, I wish to own
No palace, scepter, crown or throne,
And, being in your company,
No other place I wish to be,
Or offered of the world entire,
I have of it all I desire.

A LIFE WITH LOVE

A lonely, cold, and wasted life
Is like a dark and empty room
With days identical and blank,
Alike, and featureless with gloom.

A life with love is like a door
That opens, like a sunrise breaking,
Like the heavens shining forth,
Or like a flower to life awaking.

NORTH STAR

North star, oh beacon who desires
No other place within the sky,
But serves us as a steady light
That sailors set their courses by,
And are content in day or night
Throughout the ages, time unknown,
To share the radiance so bright
From your far celestial throne.

Grand redwood, bold and true,
Oh, symbol of a steadfast strength,
Whose roots are of enduring force
And years are of enduring length,
Who stand unmovable and sure
Like a pillar whose great
And mighty valor teaches man
To stand and never deviate.

I speak to you who understand
And whom no powers move or stir,
For I desire, admire no other
Since my heart belongs to her.

THE HIDDEN DIAMOND

With a long-accustomed eye
At many chronicles of life I've looked
And turned a chapter now and then
Until it seems a well-read book
Complete with artificial smiles
And filled with well-delivered lies
Manufactured with the wiles
That false and cunning hearts devise,
And so have learned to separate
The worthless from the genuine
And found in you a diamond hidden
In a dark and sunless mine.

NO ONE BUT YOU

When dawn unfurls above us
And reveals the morning sun
I'll waken with you in my arms
And want no other one.

When noontide vibrates with the sound
Of work and ploy and deed,
If in a team as two we toil,
No other will I need.

When dusk reclines across the sky
And stars sail into view,
You will be the world to me,
I'll want no one but you.

I LOVE YOU

I love you on the flying wings of joy
And from the darkest prison cell of grief,
When sorrow damps the slender flame of hope
You are anodyne and sweet relief;
Independent of the whims of time,
In quietness and in celebration,
I love you equally in joy or depth,
From the highest or the lowest station;
I love you in remembrance of old pain
And with the silent joy your love begets,
Nor do I still dwell on past mistakes,
Which, for love of you, my heart forgets,
With the laughs, the fears, the smiles, the tears,
In the many costumes of its breadth,
From the forward launching berth of life
To the final calling port of death,
In the empty room of solitude,
When together or when forced to part,
In the noise of day or hush of night,
Never do you venture from my heart.

TO CHERISH YOU

Nothing excels the country greens
Painting their floral country scenes
With boughs that droop when summer sighs
In breezes dancing on the skies
Or casting sundarts emanating;
So stand I at your heart awaiting.

Or when the sky surrenders light
To the call of the long, immortal night,
To the language of locust and whippoorwill,
To the chattering cricket upon my sill,
And with their evensong do I confess
To cherish you to everlastingness.

THE REST

My eyes were filled with beauties less
Before the hour I knew your face,
But since that moment they have fled
Before a more excelling grace.

One time I knew sweet melodies
That charmed the ear in flowing strains,
But since I heard your voice no other
Sound within my heart remains.

Long past I took the greatest joys
Surveying nature's rich behest,
But since I held her finest work
I can no more recall the rest.

FOR ALL THE DAYS

I want to feel you close within my arms
Until the sun ascends within the sky
And we arise to meet the toil of day,
As last night's star lights in the heavens die.

I want to love you through the hours of day,
Throughout its disappointments and its joy,
With whatsoever cards the fates shall deal
And with a love that time will not destroy.

I want to be with you when day is done
And spend my nights within your arms, to be
No more apart, but ever at your side
For all the days that life has given me.

I WISH

You are my world, my sun, my moon,
My stars, and all that is bright,
You are the best of all good things
That have ever illumined my life.

You are the one I've prayed for, dreamed of,
Waited for from the start,
And, finding you, no other will do
Since you've confiscated my heart.

You have my life, my soul, my love,
And every part of me,
I only wish to be the one
You want eternally.

THE MOMENT
I HELD YOU

I discovered the world
The moment I held you;
What once was but a dream of life
I now beheld anew,
All acquired a dazzling glow
As though a golden flood
From the very firmament
Flowed within my blood;
When your spirit touched me
As the butterfly the flower,
The part of me you took has not
Returned since that hour,
And when my heart embraced you
The glory that I knew
Swept over souls and made them one
That once before were two.

MESSENGERS

When the soulless night
Descends in shades of blue,
Casting empty shadows
Of longings borne to you,
I have but to call
Selene from her place,
And with my urgent tidings
To your side she shall haste;
Or if in morning's glow
I miss you in my arms.
And no piping songbird
Can assuage me with her charms,
I only have to summon
Aurora from the sky,
And she with my kisses
Unto you shall fly;
Or if at burning noon
I find myself alone
And my forlorn state
I begin to bemoan,
I need no more than send
My wishes high above,
Where Jupiter's bright chariot
Can bear the fires of love;
Or if in twilight's evening
I fall beneath her spell
And drowsy thoughts of you
Begin in me to dwell,

I yet can send my thoughts
Though I never leave my seat,
For Mercury shall fly to you
Upon his winged feet,
For though within another place
And in another time,
Within you my heart shall live
And love forever shine.

IF DEATH
SHOULD COME

Dear, if death should come to you
Before it comes to me,
Do not accept the summons grim
With equanimity,
Or if, perchance, death seek me first,
Then neither, dear, shall I,
For since you are my very life
I'll not consent to die.

From the thrall of age, my dear,
Yearn not to be free,
For I'll wear the selfsame yoke
And keep you company.
If not, then, for your own sake, dear,
Please wage a winning fight,
For my sake, for if you should leave
You take with you my life.

I LOVE YOU
WITH A LOVE

I love with a love of the body
That longs to hold you tight
As the fledgling day unfolds
Her destiny, the night.

I love with a love of the soul
That longs to share your plight
All the days of eternity
As dark with partner, light.

I love with a love of the spirit,
And two with a love that is one,
As the East from her mate, the West,
Can never be undone.

FINDING GODOT

Who can persuade me I've waited for nothing,
The beast in the jungle that never appears,
Who can convince me the music's not real
Simply because no other man hears,
Who can tell me that dreams come true
Only in frameworks of fairy tales,
Who can assure me the best-laid plan,
The hope of man forever fails?
Researchers know that nothing is proven,
But by provision accepted as true
Until there's a case to contradict
That which before they assumed they knew.
I don't believe the propaganda,
I don't support the campaign – no, no,
For I am the case that disproves the theory;
I've waited, you've come, and welcome, Godot.

DREAMS OF LOVE

The wind of night sings,
The warm scent of darkness clings,
Above me, as the stars overhead
Look down upon this earthly bed,
At my beating heart's request
Into your waiting arms I press.

Night is all the cover
Needed by a fervent lover
And the warming wind's caress
Mocks my passion's breathlessness;
The stars put on a show above
As we combine in dreams of love.

TRAVELER

Rest you, weary traveler,
Who've crossed the nations wide
And roamed the regions of the seas
That continents divide;
Peace, be still, consider
That that which you desire
Cannot be found though you should search
This mighty world entire,
For happy heart and joyous mind
Cannot be purchased here
And true content cannot be found
In places far or near,
The best of life's bright treasures
May only be divined
Within the climate of the heart
And landscape of the mind.

FOREVERMORE

It's such a short walk down this road,
Such a brief sail to the shore,
Such a wide world to examine
With scant time to explore.

What a vast reach rests behind us,
What a long stretch looms before;
To express how much I love you
I shall need forevermore.

HERO

You are my strong commander
Who, fearless, defeat defied
When I had forsaken hope
And faithful resolve had died.

You are my true supporter
Who, steadfast, gave love to me
When loneliness prevailed and
Despair had victory.

Then how is it a wonder,
A marvel that men brand
A mystery that none can see
And none can understand,

That you should be my hero,
My very life and breath,
For you removed my hopelessness,
A foe far worse than death.

SAGA

The rose has folded into itself,
And, tucked in its green bed,
Lies with never a restless dream
And sleeps the sleep of the dead;
The moon's come out and sails upon
A starry sea of sky
Where the moonbeams navigate
And the firefly,
Luninescent like a spark
In the inky night
Punctuates the downy dark
With fireworks of light;
The hoot owl and the whippoorwill,
With their plaintive cries,
Fill the darkness, blending with
The balmy breezes' sighs;
The drowsy jasmine's sweet perfume
Wafts upon the air
And sick again with missing you
I struggle with despair,
The fearsome dragon that waylays
And that, at last, I slay,
Though wounded, to rise up again
And then resume my way;
The minutes creep through midnight's sleep,
The dreary hour is late,
A falling star, so silent, slides,

And, weary with the wait,
I know in several hours' space
I'll clasp you close, and then,
All that's wrong within the world
Will be well again.

THE MAGNET

Snows portend the year's demise
And flowers from their glory fall
In withered shards upon the ground
When winds of autumn come to call.

Mighty kingdoms, conquerors,
In covenants with destiny,
The whims of fortune sweep aside
As lightly as the fallen leaves.

Youth, so consummate in pride,
Maintains its zenith for a time
Until it drops from summit high,
Usurped by age into decline.

You, my love, my life, my soul,
Though seasons change both you and me,
Are like a magnet, and my love
Shall follow you eternally.

DISCOURAGEMENT

The book of day is done,
The leaf of twilight turned
With the dying sun,
The court of day adjourned;
The hour waxes small,
The shadow legions come
As Silence cushions all;
The night watch has begun;
Like a black abyss,
Like a gaping grave,
Like an inky seabed,
A cavern or a cave,
The dusk has swallowed all,
And while they dozed in sleep
Descended like a pall
As dark as ocean's deep,
And though I grope my way
The hour grows so late,
Hope's a fragile flame and
The darkness is so great.

THE AWAKENING

The empty world of black and white,
Of shade and shadow that I knew
You painted o'er in colors bright
Of every kind of dazzling hue;
The world's discourse, that was but noise
And idle chatter to my ear,
You made into a melody
That everywhere I turn I hear;
The old, sad world that once I knew
Was to my eyes a weary sight,
'Till you with magic filled my heart
And I, once dead, stepped into life.

IT IS YOURS

It is yours to do with as you will,
It is yours to cherish or to break,
It is yours to love or to abandon,
But, part not with it for my sake;

It is yours to keep with you forever;
Whatever you should choose to do,
Whether to shatter or to treasure,
My heart forever will be true.

FOREVER WILL OUR LOVE BE YOUNG

Then, despot, time, come if you must
With every scourge of your domain,
For though you should require my life,
My youth and beauty shall reclaim,
For though your gray hairs tyrannize
And your infirmities must reign,
For your onslaughts I have no fear,
For your bombardments, no disdain,
For I have one I dearly love
And dearly he loves me as well,
And in our love do we possess
Sufficient power to break your spell,
For all things are subject to your
Authority excepting one,
Though we together may grow old
Forever will our love be young.

THE CARBON CHAIN

If you were an exon nucleotide
I'd be the intron at your side,
Or, if transfer RNA,
The amino acid you carried away;
If you were a winding DNA band
I'd be your complimentary strand,
Or if you were messenger RNA
With my DNA you'd interplay;
If you were a sugar, I'd pair as you base
And we'd be locked in an embrace,
Or if a nucleotide phosphate
I'd be your covalent carbon mate,
Or if you were an amino group,
And I the carboxyl type,
We might form a dipeptide bond
When we unite.
If you were an erythrocyte
And I were an eosinophil
We'd travel the bloodstream day and night
And mingle together at will;
If you were a ligand on a cell
I'd be the receptor on which you'd dwell;
If you were acetylcholine
And I a neural ganglion
You'd need but caress me
To provoke me to respond;
If we were a plasma membrane
You'd be the E face, I the P,

And, being amphipathic, we
Would live harmoniously.
If you were an enzyme,
I'd be your coenzyme,
Enfolded in your active site
Until the end of time,
Or maybe I would choose to be
Your special substrate mate,
And we would fit like lock and key
And, joined, luxuriate.
If we were two sister chromatids
Whose passion had been kindled,
We'd take a long, romantic trip
Along the mitotic spindle,
United by our centromere,
Enjoying our estate,
We'd languish on the reaches of
The metaphase plate.
If you were a nucleus
And I a chromosome,
I'd forsake the cytoplasm,
Seeking you alone;
And, leaving life, we shall not sever
But continue on together.
If you are carbon in the atmosphere
I'll be the air that holds you near,
Or as bicarbonate in the sea,
Dissolved, we'll snuggle, roaming free,
Or if you end as carbonate
We'll settle together in some lake,
And finishing as dolomite,
Solidified, I'll hold you tight,

Or lifted again above the sea,
Together, erode naturally,
Travel down some rolling stream,
Through someone's tap we'll flow unseen,
And boiled in their kettles, here
As residue we'll reappear;
Or finishing as coal or oil,
Together in some piston toil,
And then back to the gaseous state,
Where you shall still remain my mate;
With whate'er shape you are endued
My feelings never shall occlude,
Whate'er your place in the carbon chain,
My love for you shall still remain.

ONE

The beat of the track taking me back,
The flash of the passing sign,
The long, sleek rail like a comet's tail
And the sheet of slate-gray sky;
The hum of the rail and the wooded dale
As the train goes rocking by,
The home-lined street in its Sunday sleep
As travelling home am I;
Magnified against the sky,
The cityscape growing near,
The silver thread of riverbed
And passing boats appear;
A single voice in a world of choice
I wait alone to hear,
Of a million sum I long for one
As the train conducts me near.

THE TREASURE

As within a humble oyster's shell
A pearl hides,
Within a pitchy gorge of mine
A gleaming gem abides,
As the night sets off the stars
Which can't be seen by day,
I found a star more bright than those
Which in the heavens stray;
I found a pearl far dearer than
All of those that sleep
Within the murky chasms of
The ocean's shadowed deep,
And as a shining diamond hides
Within the darkest mine,
I found your smile, a treasure of
A far, far brighter kind.

MY HEART

My heart saw you,
And like a careless tide,
Your presence swept over me,
Washing all other thoughts aside.

My heart heard you,
And as March brings
Gusts, your voice enveloped me,
And I, from then, could hear no other thing.

My heart was touched,
And like the sun's light,
The warmth of your arms around me
Made all other things appear as night.

TIME

Like a meteor in space,
Like a sunbeam's speedy pace
Or as the unrestricted wind
Our hours together seem to race;

Endless as eternity,
A rock's erosion by the sea
Or evolution's slow ascent
Our hours apart appear to me.

Look at that indifferent clock,
It sits there, such a smug device,
Intoning with its pulse of quartz
A beat so maddeningly precise;

I watch its contradicting hand
Expose my heart's deceitful game;
When hours seems so relative,
How dare it say they're all the same?

A THOUSAND WAYS

If I knew the language of the trees
And could interpret every foreign phrase
They whisper to the love-enamored breeze
I'd say I need you in a thousand ways.

If I spoke the dialects of the heart
Or could sing the passions as they do,
If I could voice the feelings they impart
Every line would say, I love you.

TO LIE AT NIGHT

To lie at night, aware that I am loved,
Warmed, content, consoled within your arms,
To turn, and find you sleeping next to me,
Sheltered from the world and all its harm;

For morning's sun to fall on our embrace
And stir the love so deep we both concede,
To have the one who made my life complete
Is all within this world I'll ever need.

THE MINER

Who owns the charter of the day,
And who can spend the currency of the sun?
I am but a sometime tenant here
Who borrows shares of beauty on the run.

Who is the possessor of a heart,
Who commands the destiny of man?
I am but a humble miner here,
Who searches for its ore within my pan.

WITHIN MY HEART, WITHIN MY MIND

Is it any wonder that
I look but I no longer see
The beauty of the earth and sky,
Of nature's wealth surrounding me
For when I view the icy stars,
The aqua mountains of the sea,
The cliff-sheer drop from summit's top,
The dawn's unflowering majesty,
The early dew upon the field
Before the bright sun's rays break through,
My eyes observe but cannot see
For all my heart beholds is you,
Where, in my thoughts, you constant live,
The occupant of all my time,
For every last recess you fill
Within my heart, within my mind.

MAN

The early morning sun comes flickering
Through the sprigs' and leaflets' green,
With shadows shifting, darting, quickening,
As a wild, exotic dream,
And focuses on each performer
Spotlights made of shimmering sun
And favors every virtuoso
With a halo, golden spun;
Then, with curiosity,
The wind descends to join the show,
Rippling and jostling,
Wailing high and whispering low,
Swaggering on to play her part,
Strutting like a reigning queen,
Capturing the hardest heart
And deftly stealing every scene,
'Till down declines the screen of night;
They vanish swift as they began
As though they'd never been, so like
That other actor, known as man.

ALONE

The world can care, dear, for itself
And seems to get along just fine
Without you, for its laws obey
Some master plan and grand design;
The sun arises, night descends,
From cloud the snows and showers fall,
The earth in winter falls asleep
And wakens when the springtime calls,
So don't be too concerned for it,
The world is well and getting by
Alone, but when you're far away
From me, how miserable am I.

THIS FORTRESS

This fortress grand and glorious
With might and majesty refined,
This structure true and worthy, with
The greatest artistry designed,
With time's torments and age's wear,
When storm assaults and winds assail
Though worn with years shall stand erect,
A shelter that shall never fail,
Much as we, when years compile
Shall each unto the other provide
A haven safe of loving arms
In which forever we'll abide.

BUT FOR A DAY

If you were me but for a day
And saw the world as from my eyes,
If you could walk within my steps
Then you should know, and not surmise;

If you could step within this flesh
And feel my feelings, you would see
How very deeply you are loved,
If for a day you could be me.

FRAGILE LIFE

Fragile as butterflies' wings,
As the lark's song fading and dying,
The fortunes of men drift downstream
Soon after the rising.

Courtiers taste of fame
And then secede their power,
As with a downcast head they fall
As does the wilted flower.

All bright deeds, and dark
Give way to anonymity;
The candle's flame and rainbow's glory
Fade with equanimity.

And men's vain hopes which like
An evanescent light
Plummet like a fallen star
Into the endless night.

LESSONS

Look at the lessons all around us,
The bud that is wooed with the kiss of the bee,
The creatures of earth and sky and ocean
That pair, two by two, symbiotically,
The woodlands that wait a long night
For the appearance of the sun,
The rivers that from their separate paths
Converge with a thrust and become one,
The meadowlands whose sunny slumber
Is freshened with visits of Spring shower,
The tossings and frolics and teasings of wind
On flower cavorting with neighbor flower,
And high above the flirting of
The winds that court across the sky
With brushings and claspings of the clouds
That meet and mingle, whisking by,
And in the deep of ocean's sleep
The urgent currents of the sea
That come together, joined in mirth,
To dance a merry revelry,
For all of these in pairs belong
Nor ever pause to question why,
But unite in coupled love
As naturally as you and I.

SECOND TO YOU

Oh, the storm of a hectic life,
Equal parts of chaos and strife,
Earning a living, buying bread,
Supplying staples of board and bed,
Papers to write, books to read.
The toll exacted to succeed,
A home to keep and food to cook
And upkeep can't be overlooked,
Traffic stalemates to and fro
To fence with, ever on the go,
And don't forget a mite of pleasure
Meted in for good measure,
Dreams by thousands locked in queue,
One and all, second to you.

THE QUESTION

I asked the sun, where is he,
The one whose heart is hid in me,
But, with his golden halo spun,
He never paused upon his run.

I questioned of the vagrant moon,
Will he return to my arms soon,
But she spoke only silence so
From her confidings I'll not know.

I asked the stars so high above
To tell me of the one I love,
But they could merely stare and shine;
From them I'll not receive a sign.

Perhaps, then, all these luminaries,
Asked of you, seem so contrary,
For they see a brighter one
Whose loveliness compares with none.

And so I have but to endure
The last forever you've been gone,
The endless days when I am sure
That all the world and life are wrong,

Until we hold each other tight,
Rejoicing, you return to me,
And all the world and life are right
And I laugh at adversity.

IF THE SUN
COULD SEE

If the sun could see
And on the earth espy,
I know that she would borrow from
The dazzle of your eye;
And if the sea could speak
The musings of its mind
Your voice's melody would bear
Its message to mankind;
Or if the wind had form
Or loveliness or grace,
I know that she would choose to wear
The semblance of your face;
But if the world could feel,
So taken it would be
With your exquisite loveliness
That's all that it would see.

YOUR SMILE

Your smile is a bright bouquet
Of warmth and love and joy and light
That like the flowers of the field
Enchants and captivates my sight.

Within your eyes there lives the dawn
That as a prism in the sky
Shows every shade of wonderment,
Of happiness each hue and dye,

And in your heart the very world
With magic and delight abounds
Where tenderness as infinite
As all the universe resounds,

For in your heart and in your smile,
In every thought and word and deed
Is every dream I ever dreamed
And all within this world I need.

THE SUBSTANCE
OF A DREAM

Life, the substance of a dream,
Life, the observance,
A sleep and a sleep between,
Life, whatsoever it may mean,
As a stream not long, a lake not deep,
Is a fragile essence, a conjured charm,
A magic spell contrived of belief,
An imposter alliance with death, the thief,
That dissipates swift, as it was invoked,
For a moment swells, and flags as soon,
To which we mortal souls are yoked,
But then at last freed from the flesh,
In an otherworldly rest,
Released from a spell that cannot last,
The efflorescence that fades so fast.

SURRENDER

Ever since I first espied him
All about me, where I look,
Ever since, so long beguiled,
I see his face in nature's book;
This alchemy of golden hair
Is sunshine's echo, yet more fair,
Elixir's magic, such a hue
No daffodil can hope to share,
And if I chance to look upon
The starry-plummaged midnight sky,
I see the selfsame shade of blue
I once discovered in his eye,
And when I gently feel the wind,
Besiege my hair or graze my arm.
I cannot but recall his touch,
So soft, so gentle, and so warm,
And seeing him wherever I look.
It is not liberty I seek,
As you'd suppose, but even that
My dotage should become complete.

No place too far

No place too far, no time too long,
No journey's reach too wrought with fear
Before the bell's memorial
Intones my final moment here;
'Ere the summons to another
World, where waits another shore,
Before I'm called to venture through
That portal's great and unmarked door,
I seek a destination, and a
Distant dream do I pursue;
Although it takes a lifetime's measure,
I shall search a lifetime through,
And when through toils and lonely strife
I begin to near the place,
I shall know I have arrived
When I at last discern your face.

WITHOUT YOU

There is a light within my room;
Then why is it so dark?
Within the lampshade's golden glow
The room looks cold and stark;
Twelve hours have passed since eight o'clock
And yet the clock strikes ten;
The hands maintain a steady pace
But time stands still again,
And though the days and nights revolve
They all are turned to gray;
I exist but do not live
And time erodes away.

New Year

"Hail the new year," call the horns;
The streets resound with shouts and cries
And colored costumes fill the night
With fireworks as the old year dies.

This, the calendar decrees,
Must be the long-awaited day
Whose honored undertaking is
To see the new year underway,

But yet it is no different than
The common days we give no due,
A simple, arbitrary date
That signals that the year is through;

For every moment of our lives
Is like a newly sighted shore
And every hour we encounter
We have never seen before,

And if I were to give an hour
Tribute of eternal fame,
'Twould be the hour that we first loved,
From which my life's no more the same.

THE COMPASS

When you turn your steps afar
Upon the quadrants of the world
And find your paths most distant-aimed
Like comets through the cosmos hurled,
When all about you's strange and new,
Removed so from my arms and home,
Although exploring unknown climes
You feel loveless and alone,
I ask you then to turn your eyes
Above, upon the star-filled sky,
Observing there the North star's light,
For such a constant source am I,
A steady, true, and fixed mark
From which lost travelers find their way;
As this am I, a faithful love,
To which you may return someday,
And as a compass turns true north,
When you have tired and voyaged long,
My love awaits your safe return
Within these arms, where you belong.

REPETITIONS

Did ever wind run short of breath
With one great gust and die;
One spring must follow on another
With his autumn nigh;
Each wave gives way to his brother,
Mingling with the sea,
And rushes on to meet the shore,
Then may you not meet me?
All Nature's world repeats itself,
Flower succeeding flower,
Then may we save from out her ages
But a single hour?

What if the sun had scaled night
But once to bring the day,
And loathe to make the journey twice
In useless splendor lay;
No river ceases in its flow
Or leaves from forging ever –
Should we then not take heed of these,
Once would preclude never.

SEPARATION

The sun forsakes the sky each day,
The moon takes leave, but they return;
Then why, accustomed to departures,
When you journey, do I yearn?

We've but one sun and but one moon
That light the sky by day and night
And I have but one love in you
Within my world, the single light.

But earth waits patiently for dawn
As groom awaits a glorious bride;
Though I know you must venture forth,
Not death itself can love divide.

NATURAL LOVE

Within the airy void the robins fly
And fish disport themselves within the sea;
The mammals roam the regions of the land,
Each species seeks its place accordingly;
Electrons find their proper orbital
And atoms bind together into place,
While molecules form objects of the world
And worlds arrange themselves in outer space;
We find an order in this universe,
A plan and pattern in all things designed,
As in the substance of your love for me,
The purpose of my life I have divined,
For when your arms enclose me in the dark
As we in sleep surrender to the night
I know at last that this is why I live,
To share our love, so natural and right.

THE LOVE WITHIN

And if I write your name upon the hours
And feel the steady increment of time,
Or watch the summer's flowers' petals fall
And see the seasons rise but to decline,
I know that if I cast my love in words
As well they might be drawn upon a wave
Or writ upon the scroll of fickle wind
Or on the parchment of the sands engraved,
For time shall turn our empires back to clay
And they shall lose who've placed in man their trust,
The years will soon relentlessly transform
The heart that loves, the hand that writes, to dust;
Since monuments erode and monarchs fall,
Since fame is frail, what lasting may I give?
Though flesh will fail I give the love within
As long as life within this soul shall live.

BUT ONE YOU

So many faiths, so many creeds,
So many paths for destinies,
How many souls, how many treasures,
Countless sorrows, countless pleasures.
How numberless the grains of sand
And blades of grass that green the land,
So many stars to fill the sky
There seems no end to Heaven's supply,
How great the bounty of the sun
Whose warmth suffices everyone,
How vast a framework is the sky,
How many clouds disport on high,
How many harbors, many homes,
And crevices the wild wind roams,
As many waves as ply the shore
There lies no end to ocean's store,
How wide a space eternity,
How vast a room infinity,
How many-faced this creature, man,
His births and deaths since time began.
With all this rich world's revenue,
How strange my heart finds but one you.

WEALTH

We may not dress in finery,
Our garments may be old,
But yet our love shall still be new
When others have grown cold.
We may not boast of diamonds, gold,
And pearls in our possession,
But we'll be rich as kings in warmth
And wealthy in affection,
And what the time of age has tarnished,
What the years have worn,
Will look as bright as if brand new
With happiness adorned,
So doubt all else, believe one thing,
That this I pledge is true,
Forever you will be my king
And I adoring you.

Λ MOMENT

Within the confine of his bed
The man who draws his final breath
Discovers but a moment lies
Between the realms of life and death;
The dark infinity of night
Before the sky erupts in dawn
Seems measureless, 'till floods of golden
Light appear, and it is gone;
Within an instant does the storm
With all its fury pass away,
And all the heavens are aglow
Which wore a mask of sullen gray;
So seems my life, for on the sorrows
Of the past I'll think no more,
For in your love I found my life
As though I never lived before.

SUSTENANCE

Of all the nations of the world
And all its cities great and small,
Of all the peoples it contains
There lives but one among that all,
Whom out of every sort and kind
That dwell within this world entire,
I so with all my powers love
And I with all my heart desire,
And that one love, with all my strength
I hence shall ever strive to please
Until by death I'm taken from
That one whom I so deeply need,
For like the rain to thirsting flower
And nectar to the searching bee,
Or manna to a hungering man,
Your kiss is sustenance to me.

SILENT PEACE

Singing bird and swaying tree
And no responsibility,
Lazy-drifting mirrored stream,
Enchantment like a sweet daydream
With floating boat all lily-flanked
And tapered emerald grassy bank;
Seed in summer-scented air
Lands by nodding flower, where
With nectar, vivid blossoms tease
The summer-maddened, doting bees;
Upon my lap you rest your head,
Observing reed-lined riverbed,
With dipping oar and glinting lake;
Behind, the murmur of the wake
Like a half-remembered song,
Like the charm of childhood gone;
We ask no more than one another
In this land of summer slumber
Where the world is silent peace,
And from our cares we find release,
For heaven scarce could find a way
To fashion a more perfect day.

CONTENT AS ANY KING

If I have no mansion,
No riches and no gold,
My dwelling is uncertain
And my clothing old,
If I wear no laurels,
If I claim no wealth,
If I wear no honors,
Yet I count myself,
Though, save for you alone,
I have no other thing,
Prosperous as a prince,
Content as any king.

ALL I EVER WANT TO BE

In wishing I might wish myself
The bearer of a handsome mien,
And graced with virtues brilliant as
The brightest any world has seen,
Or I might wear a scholar's cap,
Distinguished author of a tome,
Or leave a monument of words
Within a masonry of poem,
Perhaps I'd be a businessman
Walking in success and wealth
Or else request longevity,
A cheerful mind, long life, and health,
Or I might ask an artist's fame
With scores of fans outside my door,
Or, having all of this, I'm sure
That, thinking, I would wish for more,
But as my humble, simple self,
If you should deign to care for me,
I have my dearest wish come true,
I'm all I ever want to be.

THE VIRTUOSO

You are a rock to which I cling
When storms of life appear,

A window upon the vista'd world
That beckons me ever near;

You are the virtuoso who
Teases a song from life

And I the listener in whom the song's
Transformed into delight.

Into Your Arms

Listen to the slow clock's pace;
It seems to mock the beating of my heart,
A cadence that I've learned so well
To tabulate the hours we're apart.

Hear how the raindrops descend;
They trickle and they glide down my pane,
With patience see their journey to its end,
As I wait to see you again.

Look how the sunflower turns
Her face, ever faithful, ever true,
To follow after her beloved sun,
As my feelings journey unto you.

Mark how the powers of the night
Lead the moon in darkness through the sky,
And as the sun bursts forth upon the dawn
Into your waiting arms I shall fly.

FORGIVE, MY LOVE

Forgive, my love, this wretched fool
From whom a newer woman's born,
Although her back, for that hard rod,
Is bleeding and is torn;
You ran for me; now I shall run
Although the race is very long;
The love you gave shall lift me up
When legs grow weak that once were strong;
Again I shall regain the prize
Regardless of the pain or cost,
That once was mine, unrecognized,
That through my blindness I had lost,
And when my race is at an end,
Which, God be with me, I shall win,
I'll lose myself within your arms
And my life shall begin.

HERO

My hero's not within a book,
A dark and brooding swain who dwells
Atop a windswept seaside cliff
Above the beating ocean's swells;
My hero's not upon the screen,
A suave and mustached rogue who'll seize
The hearts of damsels, make them swoon,
And duel the villains to their knees;
My hero doesn't walk a stage
To make admirers laugh and weep
Or sing a song, an idol to
The fans who gather at his feet;
My hero lives within my life,
And in his arms I make my home,
For there resides within his love
The greatest wealth I've ever known,
And when he smiles, so smile his eyes,
That shine as brightly as his mind;
While strong and sovereign with the world,
With me so caring, warm, and kind,
He strives to hide a loving heart
Which speaks and cannot be concealed,
And, shy of feelings, touchingly,
His reticence their truth reveals,
And when he speaks no gloom remains,
The shadows shy and run away,
His eyes my world light, and darkness
Cannot coexist with day.

A DIALOGUE

"Hail to the conquering chief,"
The people say, "He'll bring relief
From famine, war, and tyranny;
At lasts the masses shall be free.
No time as this has ever been
Within the history of men,
Where all shall prosper, joyous, free,
And govern democratically. "

"But no," another voice has said,
The echo of the planet's dead,
"We've witnessed many a revolution,
Yet the ultimate solution
Never will nor can be found
As long as human hearts abound
With hatred, greed, corruption, lust;
No rulership is ever just,
And that same man who represents
An answer to our discontents,
Before his term is at an end,
Becomes the fool we've all condemned,
For historians assent
From darkness to enlightenment
The world has turned, and still today
Continues so to oscillate,
Which only goes, at last, to show
The answers man shall never know,

Nor would he practice what it takes
To make the world a better place;
And those who answers hope to find
In man will find their hopes are blind. "

THE PRICE

"He sold his soul," a neighbor said,
"To gain a dream he dearly paid
With sweat and toil; he would have bled,
Never from his purpose swayed. "

"He gave his all," a friend maintained,
"He sacrificed so many things
To reach his goal, not once complained,
To reap rewards persistence brings. "

"He earned the right," another swore,
"To bask within his fortune's glow,
For what he did to reach that shore
Only those there with him know. "

"There's no doubt he paid his due
For he was purchased by his wealth;
Every word they say is true;
The price he paid was of himself."

YOU NEVER CAN BE OLD

You never can be old to me
Though you may wear the scars of time,
For I shall love you endlessly
Until the clock's departing chime,
For it is not the weary flesh
But you who look from out those eyes,
For bodies weaken day by day
And flesh is but the soul's disguise;
And it is not the raven hair
That time shall straightly turn to gray,
But the one who speaks the words
Of love that never wear away,
For we have proof, hour by hour,
That our mortal scaffolds fail
For they are merest clay, but my
Love shall evermore prevail.

THE BEACON

You are a beacon to my heart,
A landmark sighted night and day,
Which in storm or gale or dark
Never fails to guide my way.

You are a threshold to my soul,
The stile on which my lifetime turns,
A doorway that I enter through,
The aim for which my spirit yearns.

THE TRANSFORMATION

I see, I hear, I feel, I touch
As I never did before;
It seems that from the draught of life
I drink a measure more,
Was it you who worked the magic,
Genii who enchants?
The world appears a different place
To one who's so entranced.
Has it changed? No, I have changed
For nothing looks the same;
It must be so and all I know
Is I have you to blame.

THE GIFT

I would like to give to you
All things that are beautiful,
All things lovely, all things bright,
All things glorious, if I might;
I'd give you sunlight, pure and gay,
And sunsets to see off the day,
I'd give a still and snowbound night
With snow-fleeced tree and moon's pale light,
The forest's undiluted green,
The cast of creatures in its scene,
The stars, the signposts of the night,
I'd give the eagle's vectored flight,
The waves that rock, the clouds that float,
All that on which the summers dote,
The way light pierces crystalled-ice,
Fresh robust wind, blue water, bright,
I'd give you these, all these and more
From out the planet's ample store
But cannot give what isn't mine
Regardless of how rich or fine,
But what you placed inside of me
I can return as poetry,
The joy, the love, the perfect peace,
I should like to give you these,
But since words cannot show it,
Poems are yours, and the poet.

PEACE

To a life troubled with hurt,
Pierced with injuries,
To years worn with solitude
And burdened with unease,
Peace has come in the form of you,
An unexpected guest,
Bearing deep contentment
And the priceless gift of rest;
Thankful am I that
No more does spiteful grief
With relentless sorrow
Accompany my sleep,
Ever grateful, I,
That the darts of pain
With which I once was felled
Assail my heart in vain.

HAPPINESS

Happiness is not in things
But having one another,
The greatest gift the world can bring,
Supreme to any other,
Is to know the one you want
Cares equally for you,
The wisest man who lives won't find
A happiness more true.

I WILL FOLLOW YOU

O'er the echoing mountaintops,
Encrusted with a frost of white,
Across the savage, slashing sea,
Into the dark bowel of night,
Beyond the plains of solitude,
The promontories of despair,
Along the paths of penury,
Traversing trouble's thoroughfare,
Upon the endless sea of grief,
Beset with icy pangs of fear,
Where anguish knows of no relief,
When hope is far and doubt is near,
Throughout the aches and cares of life,
And then when life's forays are through,
Over the dark void of death,
Unfailing I will follow you,
No matter what the circumstance,
If with each other we are blessed,
Having one another, we
Shall never want for happiness,
And if throughout the years to come
We may with one another live,
We'll have the greatest gift that God
To mortal man shall ever give.

A GREATER WORTH

My champion, my hero,
My defender and beloved,
I would follow you through all
The darkest caverns of the night,
My fairest one, my promised,
My only love, companion,
Through Heaven's fairways I will
Walk beside you in the light,
For you are life to me,
The one I've always dreamed of,
And I of women luckier
Than all upon the earth,
To be the one upon your arm,
The one for whom you care –
This to me, than all things else,
Is of a greater worth.

I WANT TO SEE

I want to see the blue, which as
A treasure of the rarest kind
Belongs alone unto your eyes
And is within my heart confined.

I want to feel your arms around me
As the sun about the earth
Encircles her in arms of ardor,
Blessing her with daytime's birth.

I want to know, how gathered to you,
Locked together, our hearts beat,
And that exchange of feelings when
Your eyes find mine and our lips meet.

IF

If I could put my story into words
Then I could scribe the whole of history
And bring to light the origin of life,
Revealing all its secret mystery;

If words were large enough to hold it all,
Could lines contain its height and depth and length,
If sentences could cover all its size,
If paragraphs could tell of all its strength;

If book could hold a volume without end
Or statements comprehend infinity,
Then I could show the boundaries of my love
And say how much it is you mean to me.

THE CAPTIVE

How shall it be this universe,
This portal of infinity
That opens on the spangled stars
Of heaven does not so much move me
As does the simple, passing thought,
The mere remembrance of your face,
That steals my thoughts and leads my heart
A captive from its 'customed place.

And how, when I should gaze upon
The pulse of waves upon the shore
And hear the ages calling out
Eternity in ocean's roar
Can it be so that I, untouched,
At but the mention of your name
Recall no more my former thoughts
And find my world no more the same.

Or standing at the mountain's crest
Against the curtain of the sky
With worlds laid down below my feet
As though a demigod on high,
How is it so my heart seems slow,
But yet the cadence of your feet
As you approach incites my pulse
And lends my heart a racing beat.

THE KISS

A kiss, and I awaken to you
As one who comes alive,
With all before as it were no more,
From the sleep of the past revived.

A touch, and my hands announce my heart,
My eyes express my mind,
The whole of my life confesses you
And I leave the world behind.

THE EXCHANGE

Why, tell me why, is the night sky not dark
Since you've wrested the light from the moon and the stars
And placed it complete here into my heart?

And what of the world, say, how can it be
That yet it still turns, since you took it away
From its station today, and gave it to me?

But where is my heart? It is now gone away,
For you've given the sun and the stars in exchange
And I miss it no more, for with you it will stay.

ESSAYS

I placed a flower in his path,
He glanced and turned aside,
Though ne'er so little was attained
The world shall know I tried.

The notes I sowed into the song,
He scorned my suit in pride,
Though I know not how I went wrong,
The world must know I tried.

My lot I chanced and all I know
To bear him that I thought just so,
I braved, but spoke without an ear
And landed short the mark, 'tis clear.

Idle incidental, I,
A calendar long out of date,
A language locked away in time,
Slight and common trifle said he,
So he'll set me by.

If any be that hit the white,
Sweet fortune, mine, were it I,
But if my luckless aim veer wide
Safely may you say I tried.

TRANSFORMATION

In a screened porch in the early morning hours
Slides the sunlight in the stillness of her powers;
Silent comes our guest and her gift of peace.
But a thought of you translates her silence into me.

Through my window at attention stands a garrison of trees
That watch the foolish dreams of man beyond the centuries;
So fresh hopes in the youth of the heart
The sun witnesses in her flight,
But your face appears and I am converted
Into her blinding light.

FOR LOVE I
WERE A FOOL

For love I were a fool not to be a fool
With incautious age laughing in my face,
And thoughts that exceed the soul's demesne,
When I do my ceremony
Swift as lightning disembowels the sky
And touch a life but fragilely
And am gone by.

EMISSARY OF STARBEAMS

What need have I for lesser suns
That lend the mariners a course,
Or globes by which love's tales are spun
That summon tides by Mesmer's force;

Or comets that define the day
An emperor will come to rest,
Coronas that forbode a storm,
Suns that rainbows manifest,

For you are the day to my esteem;
When you are near it is not night,
Emissary of starbeams
And minister of light.

Had I but token of your store
I were rich with a thousandth part,
For your presence has my mind displaced
And overcome my heart.

MORNING SONG

To awake to the morning with you in my thoughts
And the songs that are all about,
The birds making harmonies at the sill
To the chorus of breeze without,
Backed by the brook's resonant trill
And an orchestration of trees,
The thought of you standing close to me
Brings me to my knees.
While my heart keeps time to the pace of your steps
As I hear you drawing near,
I fear it will miss its accustomed beat
When I see your face appear.
All nature rejoices with us to know
That we are sealed together;
As nature's scheme, may it always be so,
And may it abide forever.

LET ME REST
LIKE THE SUN

Let me rest like the sun
On his shining hair
And play like the breeze
On his features fair,
Let me sleep like the moon
Near his shining face
And stray like the day
Ever near his grace.

WHAT POWER DIVINE

What agency, what power divine,
What fate decreed that you be mine?
Which tea leaves or what crystal ball,
What fortune's wheel, what oracle,
What lucky charm, which stars above,
What rabbit's foot ordained our love;
I know not which detour of fate
Or cards served to prognosticate,
But lucky penny I must be
That all your love belongs to me.

NATURE'S CONSPIRACIES

Merry with the aroma of flowers
And under the spell of Spring's powers,
Madly cavorts the mischievous breeze,
Caught up in Nature's conspiracies,
Tilting the head of the asphodel,
Influenced with Spring's hypnotic spell
And playing havoc without restraint,
An artist enamored of green paint;
The earth laughs in combustions of flowers,
Then cries for their sake in life-giving showers;
Perhaps in the mirth of their celebration
They breathe and feel my anticipation,
And, as I, with their hearts beating,
Share the expectancy of our meeting.

THE HAPPIEST
OF MEN

I want to return to those arms
Where my heart lives;
I have missed it ever since
It has been his;
My soul longs to join my heart,
As waves return to shore,
To seek the face it longs to see
And leave its place no more.

As the winds of summer, racing
Sea birds down the bay,
My will inclines to meet my heart,
Where it desires to stay,
And when my heart and soul are
Together once again,
I'll be a marvel to the world,
The happiest of men.

YOUR FIRE

Last night amid the silent hours
I made love to you,
And though you'll never know, I had
The things my thoughts pursue,
For since I felt the whisper of
Your breath upon my ear,
The words you said to me that night
Are all that I can hear,
And even now I feel again
Your hair brush into mine,
Even as within my dreams
Our arms intertwine,
And still the way you took my hand
Burns within my mind
And travels through my body
As the shaft of lightning shines,
And as I lie immersed in you
And throbbing with desire
I am surrounded with your arms
And come into your fire.

YOU AND I

When you are in my arms, the world
And its disturbance ebb away,
The sun, a-wearied of its constant
Task takes leave on holiday,
The stars that burn within the night
And never-ending vigils keep
Put out their fires tonight to join
The resting planet in its sleep,
The worlds that endlessly revolve
Upon their paths about the sun
Grow restless with their 'customed course,
Requiring a halcyon,
The winds subside, the seas grow still,
Their siege upon the shore they cease,
The conflicts fade, the turmoils dim,
And everything is perfect peace,
I see unhappiness recede,
I watch despondence wane and die,
The world around us is no more,
No thing remains but you and I.

THE COUNT OF DAYS

What is the measure of devotion?
Is it numbers of tears
That quantify emotion?
The sum of imagined fears
Of being cleaved apart,
Or the volume of smiles
You compile in my heart?
Is it the amount of dreams
That future days provide?
No, it is the count of days
That I'll be at your side.

THE HERO IN YOUR SOUL

When the world is heavy upon our souls
And bows us down with grief and care,
What is this force that drives us on
To lift our heads and rout despair,
What is this voice that fortifies
Even within the grip of defeat,
When disease or famine our spirit tries,
Or death we are called upon to meet,
When some a country die defending
And lives are spilled in the clash of ideals,
What is the confidence never-ending,
What is the unknown balm that heals,
When oppressed with hatred, consumed with rage,
With breaking hearts and questioning souls,
What passion inflames the writer's page,
What light illuminates our goals,
What is it, son, we call upon
When the man within us seems to fail,
What makes our hearts and souls strive on,
What is wind to our slackened sail?

This wind is courage, courage and love,
A mighty standard, carried above,
That shall stand when others fall,
A glorious victor conquering all,
Strong and great as Damascus steel,

Although invisible, mighty and real,
And, son, when trials make you weak,
Let the inner victor speak,
When you lose faith in your high goal,
Find the hero in your soul.

PHOTOGRAPH DAYS

These are photograph days,
And this study in September
Is composed of rich displays
The beholder will remember,
The easy drift of breezes,
A vibrant flower posing,
The shy blush of bared leaves
The sun's gaze is disclosing,
The delicate flutter of jostled trees,
Sunlight on the field,
Green motility of the breeze,
The lazy languor, autumn's yield,
The dulcet murmur of the waves,
And you, a smile awaking,
Like the rich, decorous fields,
Like a sunrise breaking.

LIFE AND ETERNITY

Star serene, silent, and bright,
Like a beacon set
In the black sea of night,
That stand in place
Faithful and content,
A sentinel and signpost in
The endless firmament;

Swells that thrust upon the land,
That heave and sink and cast
Themselves upon the sand,
Know not the untold place
That they are searching for,
But ever yearn to dance and sport
Upon some distant shore;

Life, a passing scene,
A flame, a rolling stream,
Life, the shadow of
A swiftly moving dream,
In life, the measure lying
Between a mystery,
I've found the arms in which I wish
To meet eternity.

PHILOSOPHY AND LIFE

A Stroll through the Grove of Blooming

So the philosopher knows
As the bud which coffers the essence,
None the less stunted lest it grow,
Shape, ripen, burgeon
In the brilliancy of incandescent blaze,
Sunshafts paling newborn leaves, rife
In iridescent glaze of green:
So let us perform life.

ANATOMIZING

I like your dorsal
As much as your torso,
Your frontal clearly isn't bad,
Being rather contrapuntal,
I shudder at touch of your metacarpals
And in fact have known no better marvels,
Your voluntaries leave me with
A shortage in vocabulary,
The enchantment of your autonomic
Leaves me nearly catatonic,
For your medulla oblongata
I would fashion a cantata,
Your cheeks, your lips, your lovely hair
Let me know how fair is fair,
But then if they are counted nice,
They're half of what your eyes are twice,
I think as I gaze upon your sternum,
Every component, I want to learn 'em,
I would praise A through Z on your anatomy charts
But the whole is greater than the sum of the parts.

THE MOMENT THAT
MIGHT HAVE BEEN

The moment I might have
I was hurrying, worrying,
Reading, speaking,
Fighting, writing,
Eating, meeting,
Lying, crying,
Sleeping, reaping,
Resting, testing,
Starting, parting,
Smiling, riling,
The moment that might have been
I regret – a kiss.

THE DOMICILE

For such a time
You've held my mind,
I feel you've taken
Homestead there,
Your brilliant eyes
Have such an art
As plays a mischief
In my heart;
They sunder
Such a brand of light
As rivals
All the stars of night,
And I've such warmth
From these alone
I'm pleased they made
My thoughts their home.

THE OPEN DOOR

Like a warm spring breeze
The hours that have fled return to me
In such a striking, bold display
They make me think it's yesterday;
I see, by turn, passing through
The day that I took off from school
When the wind was ice and the sky was blue,
How I talked for hours without end
Of the meaning of life with an old friend;
Or how in that same winter chill
I sat in the warmth of the grill
And watched in many such times as those
The students bedecked in their colorful clothes,
Nor can I forget the brisk autumn nights
With their thumping bands and melodic delights,
But nothing remains quite as the spring
Of a dazzling, golden, sunstruck morning,
Seen from the room of an old house
Where we shared class with the resident mouse,
And casually chatted of literature while
The sun streamed in on our genial stir;
I recall the first thaw that enlivened our hearts;
By reviving her dormant magical arts,
She coaxed away old winter's care
And love was contracted on the air,
And how I remember the early dawn
With a pinkish light cast on the lawn,
And a stillness suggesting eternal places,

And hope that resides on youthful faces,
The sun that laughs down her genial powers
And teases so the sleepy earth,
Warming up her gentle flowers
Into their new springtime birth,
And I recall a smile and a wink,
Of a clasp and an invitation I think,
Of a joy that knocked upon my soul
And a heart that answered, out of control.

Λ DREAM'S LENGTH

One January night in the crisp-voiced snow
Through the bitter winds that are known to blow
In winter's prime, with our whisperings
We lulled to slumber old man time,
Two timeless hours with our charms,
Engulfed in one another's arms,
Down into the dark we fell
On that night of secrets, remembered well,
That old man time slept in our spell,
And relinquished a while his despotic powers;
For a dream's length we stilled the advancing hours.

THIS CAPTAIN

You've got some troubles dragging you down,
Some problems just won't let you be,
You feel like you're sinking in the storm,
When the sea gets rough stay close by me.

This captain goes down with the ship,
I'll stay till the water covers me,
But take my hand and we'll swim for land
And we'll both be saved from the stormy sea.

When you feel lonely and nothing goes right,
When care seems about to cover you,
So blue you cannot sleep at night,
Stay by my side and we'll make it through.

This captain goes down with the ship,
I'll stay till the water covers me,
But take my hand and we'll swim for land
And we'll both be saved from the stormy sea.

A SMILE MADE IN HEAVEN

A smile made in Heaven
Packaged and sent for me,
Is the smile upon your lips
When our glances meet.

A grace within your walk
Inspires the humblest place;
A kind of light and beauty
Accompanies your face.

You cause a special change
To overcome a room,
As when the sun outruns the clouds
And banishes the gloom.

I WHO WROTE
OF LIFE

I who wrote of life
But knew so few of its pleasures,
I who sang about love
But never tasted its treasures
Am now ashamed of lines
That were a poor deceit,
And humbled to admit my
Information incomplete,
For in a moment's breadth
Feelings never known
Overwhelmed me with a love
For you, and you alone.

ABOUT THE AUTHOR

Practicing physician Prudence Ann Smith, MD, FACR, earned her medical degree from Jefferson Medical College before completing an advanced fellowship in diagnostic radiology from the University of Wisconsin. She holds a bachelor of science degree in education from Northwestern University and did postgraduate training in English literature at the University of Illinois.

www.ingramcontent.com/pod-product-compliance
Lightning Source LLC
Chambersburg PA
CBHW060919040426
42445CB00011B/700